Agency of Change
©2013 Poppy DeBoer
Cover art ©2010 Martin Bridge, One Year of Prayer
http://thebridgebrothers.com/martinclarkbridge/
All rights reserved. Printed in the United States of America. No part of this book may be reproduced or transmitted in any form or by any means electronic or mechanical, including photocopying, recording, or by any information storage and retrieval system without the written and signed permission of the publisher.
ISBN: 978-0-9894499-0-8

for Hope

Butterflies are not just for sissies. They are not just for hippie music posters or field guides, for weddings or flower gardens. During the Holocaust, prisoners carved hundreds of butterfly images into surfaces in the concentration camps. For many cultures ranging from the Aztecs to the Irish, butterflies were the souls of the dead. The Greek word "psyche" means both soul and butterfly. Some butterfly males, such as the Zebra Longwings and the Apollos, are known to rape the females of the species. Monarch butterflies migrate as far as 3,000 miles (up to 265 miles in one day), a longer journey than many of us humans will make in our lives. They are also poisonous to predators.

Most commonly across cultures, the butterfly represents the power of transformation. We can see a caterpillar weave a cocoon around itself, lay dormant, and then suddenly emerge a whole new creature, with barely any resemblance to its former self and no corpse left behind. The butterfly has long been a Christian symbol for the death and resurrection of Christ. The Hindu god Brahma is said to have conceived reincarnation by watching butterflies.

The butterfly is probably the most universal symbol for change. This book is a collection of observations on the nature of personal transformation, and other archetypal lessons, drawn from scientific facts about butterflies, as well as poetry and myths for inspiration. It is for those who are drawn to learn spiritual lessons from the world around us, and for those who seek change, for themselves and for our world. It is for those who itch intangibly, knowing that something needs to change.

But be warned: the caterpillar does not just put on some make-up. True transformation is a kind of death, a dissolution of the old that precedes creation of the new. The butterfly's bright and beautiful colors can distract us from remembering the often frightening depths to which we must descend if we are to fully transform.

There are other lessons to be learned from the butterfly as well, lessons that may be lighter and easier than a total reconfiguration of the self. The different chapters of this book are intended to appeal to the range of potential butterflies attracted to it. You don't have to go through a death and rebirth, memorize the facts, or even enjoy the poetry. As I wouldn't expect a butterfly to feed on every kind of flower in my garden[1], I don't

---

[1] The largest swarm of butterflies I have ever seen was perched at the edge of a pool of

expect you, the reader, to delight in every single word written here. Flutter from chapter to chapter, idea to idea. Enjoy this book as you wish.

> "I will try to cram these paragraphs full of facts
> and give them a weight and shape
> no greater than that of a cloud of blue butterflies."
> ~Brendan Gill

---

liquid feces swelling up from a cracked septic pit. So even if this book seems like a big pile of poop at first, you may find something useful in one or another of the chapters.

Most creation stories say that, in the beginning, there was Nothing. Or Darkness. Or the Void. None of that is true, for there has always been Everything. And before our world existed as it does, there was only Everything, one force indistinguishable from itself.

Most creation stories say that first was created Light, or Darkness. Or Water, or the Gods. This also is not true. Everything's first creation was actually Butterfly, and this is how it happened.

Everything got so bored of being everything that it created Other. And then there was Duality – everything and nothing, light and dark, chaos and order. But that sudden separation into opposites hurt Everything. Everything felt lost and alone for the first time, unable to relate with its created opposite. So it created a third entity, Center. Now the opposites could meet and connect and relate. And those huge wings of Everything and Other, connected through the first body of the Center, started to flap and flutter, and Time and Space and Motion were created. The first butterfly was coming into being.

But its wings still were out of harmony, being total opposites. So Everything pondered, and then changed up those wings. Everything made itself part of both wings, one side of them, and made its Opposite both undersides. Now the wings were connected through the Center, and each wing shared Everything and Other. The Center began to create Heart and Joy. From the four new sides of the wings came Air, Fire, Water and Earth. And from all of these parts, the World as we know it was created.

And you can still see the beginnings of Creation in the butterfly's multi-colored wings, its erratic flight, and the joy it brings to the world.

Change and Construct

The primary lesson to be learned from the butterfly is that **change is inevitable**. Everything changes: our bodies, emotional states, goals, personalities, wardrobes, appetites, desires, ideas, beliefs, memories, friendships, finances, homes, luck, careers, habits, cultures, societies, governments, forests, oceans.

I challenge you, in this moment, to think of something that doesn't change - ever. But keep in mind, for things that seem like they don't change, to expand the scope of time. Eventually, a diamond will degrade. Eventually, a mountain will crumble into the sea. Eventually, your husband will take out the trash. Or die. (Hopefully not by your hand.)

If you thought of something like death or time, or the laws of physics, consider that these are forces of change themselves, which act upon us and our universe. They are not unchanging, because they are change.

It could be argued that change is unchanging, as it is said that "change is the only constant." But can we really say that change is unchanging, when it **is** change, which is its sole purpose and expression?[2]

Ultimately, change is inevitable, in every known realm of existence.

Therefore, its potential is accessible to anyone. Beyond solar power, love, or Murphy's Law, **change is the most sustainable and unlimited source of energy.** It is constantly present in every aspect of our lives, so we only need to figure out how to form a relationship with it.

A relationship with change is useless, however, without understanding its partner, construct. Our culture tends to have a dualistic mindset from which we perceive the world as composed of dueling opposites: good versus evil, black and white, us against them, love or hate. I would like to propose a different perspective on change and construct, more in alignment with the Chinese yin-yang. This classic symbol represents complementary opposites that are interconnected and give rise

---

[2](Inhale) Whoa, dude.

to each other, and it is commonly understood that everything has both yin and yang qualities. So we will look at change and construct as intimately necessary to the other, as partners in an eternal dance.

Construct, in its form as a noun, means the equivalent of structure and has the prefix "con-" which in Latin means "together" in the spirit of this partnership we are examining. A construct is, basically, just about anything and everything that is not a force of change.

Consider for a moment that all matter is composed of patterns within patterns. For example, this book is composed of thoughts and ideas, organized into chapters, formed by paragraphs, made up of sentences, containing words, which are arrangements of letters, printed in ink on paper, which are organic components made of molecules, which are atoms combined into patterns, and so on.

Something less objective or tangible is still a construct. For example, a personal relationship is composed of behaviors, beliefs, neurochemistry, and feelings, all of which can be dissected into layers of patterns within patterns. Just because something is a pattern, it is not necessarily predictable, as we have probably all observed in our relationships. But it is definable, whereas change is much more difficult to define, other than to say that one construct became another construct. Even if we minutely examine the changes a burning book undergoes to become a pile of ashes, we are still naming states of being, or observations of energy and matter, which are all constructs shifting from one to the other. We are unable to say what change is, other than a shift from construct to construct, however infinitesimally.

So everything besides change is a construct. Construct is patterns within patterns, the structure holding together reality itself, on every level, in every realm

I suppose one could still choose to see change and construct in warlike conflict with each other, such as dynamiting (change) a building (construct), or in the death and decomposition of a human body, but I'd like to point out that in both (and most other) cases, change hasn't really "won." There is now a construct of "rubble" which can change again into the site for a new building, or a construct of "compost" which can host and grow all kinds of bugs and plants.

Very similar to the concepts of change and construct are those of chaos and order, but our American culture wants to see chaos as "bad" and order as "good" and believe that order must somehow triumph over chaos. We seem to place value on longevity, such as calling a business successful the longer it lasts or a failure if it's only for a few years, and we have this idea that somehow permanence is obtainable and a mark of total success. Besides being really boring, this worship of order and fear of chaos doesn't really reflect the natural world around us. And systems that are built to incorporate the fluctuations of chaos, such as buildings designed to ride and survive earthquakes, tend to have more longevity than those that fight or deny it. These two forces of change and construct are the inseparable foundations of reality itself.

A construct cannot become anything different, and nothing new can grow, without change. And change has nothing to work upon without the existence of construct.

So I will continue to maintain the perspective that change and construct are in a constant dance with each other, a flow back and forth, but you are welcome to see them as battling if you wish. Or to blame butterflies for hurricanes.[3]

In summary:

Construct is the playground for change – informing it, channeling it or resisting it.

Change acts on construct – altering it, destroying it, and forming it.

Change is dynamic, and construct is static.

Change is not good or bad, nor is construct.

---

[3] In 1961, Edward Lorenz was working with a meteorological computer model, and by inputting an infinitesimally different number in one early sequence, caused an entirely different weather pattern. This became known as the Butterfly Effect, from his 1972 presentation "Does the flap of a butterfly's wings in Brazil set off a tornado in Texas?" The butterfly was a poetic improvement upon his original choice of a seagull. But it has resulted in some poorly placed blame, I feel, upon butterflies.

Life is the dance of change and construct.

"Is it sin, which makes the worm a chrysalis,
and the chrysalis a butterfly,
and the butterfly dust?"
~ Max Muller

If you have a wish, and you want it to come true, you must whisper it to the right creature, who will take it to the Creator. Just speaking your secret aloud, the wind will seize it and carry it away, and whisper it to anyone who is listening. So don't tell it to the wind.

Don't whisper your wish to the creatures of the sea. They will take it down, down, down, to the Lords of the Deep, who know nothing of human things. Your wish will become lost forever in the dark.

Don't tell your wish to any of the creatures that walk or crawl the earth. They can't reach the sky where the Creator's cloud home floats. Besides, even if the squirrels don't chatter away your wish to everyone else, they will bury it in the ground and may even forget where it is. The coyotes will tell everyone and laugh and laugh and laugh at your stupid wish. The snakes don't even care about it.

Definitely don't tell your wish to the Trickster, no matter how much he swears he is Creator's best friend! Your wish may survive his bumblings, his mad tea parties, and his fantastical lies, but even if he remembers to give it to the Creator, it will arrive torn and stained with drool. And Creator will be suspicious of it anyway.

You must tell one of the flying creatures your wish. But not the birds, because everyone knows that all birds are liars. Especially crows, who would cackle with the coyotes. Flies would drag your wish through poop and rotting garbage. Mosquitoes and bats would suck it dry.

Whisper your wish to the butterfly. It was struck dumb and humbled by the Creator for its pomposity. So don't worry, the butterfly will not tell your wish to the flowers. It may take a few days, but that butterfly will take your wish up to the Creator, who loves it still so much, and Creator will read your wish in its wings, in its flight. And Creator will smile and smile.

Inviting Change

If you're reading this book because you feel stuck or stagnant, don't worry – change is inevitable. But it's not always easy. Afflictions like depression, chronic pain or poverty can be difficult to change. And often we are not able to even articulate or point to what it is that needs to change in our lives. We just know that something isn't right, and it's slowly eating at us.

Well, congratulations. Just picking up this book is a way of taking the first and most important step in the journey of change – acknowledging that something needs to change. No matter what you think that may be, these secret teachings of the butterfly can help.

Now, this is not one of those books that claims that you can cure a terminal illness just by wishing hard enough, or that suggests you have created your own illness and that it's only your lack of faith or insight that keeps you from healing. That kind of attitude doesn't seem to really help anyone[4], and can do just as much damage to our spirits as illness itself. This book will offer some different perspectives on personal transformation, and of course, best wishes for everyone who is suffering.

Also be aware that the change you think you need may not be the change you get. Consider the famous serenity prayer: "Grant me the serenity to accept the things I cannot change, the courage to change the things I can, and the wisdom to know the difference."[5]

Yes, it's true: there are some things in life that we cannot change. But we can always change ourselves in response to them. And there are few things about ourselves that we cannot change. We can change our attitudes, behaviors, gender expression, hair, skin, beliefs, careers, minds, and social circles. We can change just about anything. And, as it is said, if you want to change the world, change yourself first.

So, having taken the first step in acknowledging that you wish a change in your life, the next step is to open to change. The most difficult

---

[4]Except for all those authors making money from their books that basically are saying "If you just wish hard enough it will come true" and "If your life still sucks you are just not wishing hard enough".

[5]Or, "the wisdom to hide the bodies of those I had to kill to do it."

obstacle for change is being closed to it. Whether it is a closed heart or a closed mind, a closed door or a closed wallet, change cannot occur without opening the way. And if change is inevitable, wouldn't you rather open the door than have it ripped off its hinges?

We can pray, meditate, or reflect on being open and receptive to whatever change needs to occur. Are you willing to be challenged to open the places in you that are closed, resistant, stuck or ignorant?

"Happiness is a butterfly, which when pursued,
is always just beyond your grasp,
but which, if you will sit down quietly, may alight upon you."
~Nathaniel Hawthorne

One day Caterpillar was minding her own business, munching leaves and soaking up sunlight, when Trickster wandered by.

"Why hello, Patercillar," said Trickster.

"Hello, Trickster," said Caterpillar, sighing. Everyone knew that Trickster carried mischief in his pockets and was impossible to ignore.

"A fine day to die, is it not?" said Trickster, giggling like gas bubbles through swamp mud. Caterpillar stopped chewing.

"Whatever do you mean?" she asked. Her skin itched.

"Why, I have it on the highest authority," spouted Trickster, "that today you are going to die, and become a Flutterby. Well, I really must be going," he said, and hurried off.

"What is a Butterfly?" wondered Caterpillar. She was disturbed and perturbed, so she decided to visit the Seven Fates and ask them. Caterpillar swung through the forest on her silk ropes to the darkest part, where the Fates lived.

"Seven Fates, Seven Wise Fates," she said. "Trickster told me that I would die today, and become a Butterfly. Do you know the truth of this? Can you see the truth in your rainbow hearts?" They nodded, every one of them, and began to speak.

"If you choose to become a Butterfly," said the First Fate, "your body will turn to water, but you will feel no pain. Then your waters will become a beautiful winged creature, and you will live the rest of your days sipping the sweet nectar of flowers."

"You will feel the greatest terror you have ever known," continued the Second Fate, "and after, the greatest joy."

"You will no longer simply eat and eat," said the Third, "but you will feed the flowers and the fruits and the trees."

"If you choose to become a Butterfly," said the Fourth Fate, "you will no longer be alone. You will travel great distances with a family of Butterflies, and see distant lands."

"Your beauty will inspire many," said the Fifth, "and some will capture you and pin you behind glass so they may witness you for all of their remaining days."

"They will be fascinated by you," continued the Sixth, "for your metamorphosis will be a mystery they wish to comprehend. They will study you and follow you to the ends of the Earth."

"You will teach them the greatest lessons of all," said the Seventh Fate, "that there is no Death, and that Fear can blossom into Joy."

"If you choose, if you choose, if you choose," chanted the Seven Fates.

And what do you think she did?

The Seven Realms of Change

Whether or not you know the change you need to make in your life, you can invite it by making change in other areas of your life. This principle is known and practiced in many cultures across the world, under different concepts or turns of phrase: sympathetic magic, you reap what you sow, what goes around comes around, or like attracts like.

For example, Christian communion is the consumption of wine and wafer, a physical act, in order to renew the adherent's relationship with Christ, spiritually. Another example would be the voodoo doll, an invention that has nothing to do with the actual religion itself, but one whose principle can be found in many cultures that utilize magic. Stabbing or burning or burying a small effigy hurts or kills the person whose hair or clothes adorn it.

Not all examples of this basic principle are religious in nature. Have you ever known anyone to cut their hair after a break-up? Or have you burned a photograph or love letters to forget someone? A picture of the new car you want, posted on your bedroom wall, or saying self-affirmations to your reflection every morning in the bathroom mirror, could be seen as an example of this principle.

The goal of this chapter is not to turn you into a witch doctor or new age devotee, but to demonstrate the breadth of the principle of like attracting like. If you wish to invite change into your life, you can start by introducing it into any and all of the seven realms. They provide a simple map of reality, which I have found useful in many applications, from starting a business to analyzing the facets of a challenging problem.

These are the seven realms:

Physical: Bodies, clothes, homes, environment

Emotional: Senses and sensuality, feelings and moods, desires, personal space

Active: Habits and routines, physical labors, willpower

Relational: Culture, circle of friends, relationships

<u>Expressive</u>: Communication, language, the creative process

<u>Mental</u>: Thoughts, beliefs, morals, scientific observations

<u>Spiritual</u>: Faith, divine presence, the ineffable

These layers are not meant to be exclusive of each other. For example, playing the violin would have an aspect of each one of the seven. But, using the seven realms as a lens, we would consider each facet of playing the violin separately – the creative process, the emotional impact, the discipline necessary, et cetera.

So if the challenge you are facing in life is depression, you might consider making changes in any or all of the seven realms, such as...

<u>Physical</u>: Paint your bedroom bright yellow, change your diet, clean your house.

<u>Emotional</u>: Watch comedies or comedians to laugh more, get a massage (not *that* kind).

<u>Active</u>: Go for a long walk in nature every day, quit drinking alcohol, take a dance class.

<u>Relational</u>: Talk with a good friend, hang out in coffee shops, join a discussion group.

<u>Expressive</u>: Sing in the shower, paint with watercolors, make a superhero costume for grocery trips.

<u>Mental</u>: Read books for children, attend a workshop, research common causes of depression.

<u>Spiritual</u>: Meditate on being your spiritual hero, attend an unusual religious service.

If you are trying to quit smoking, you might quit going to places where people smoke, start an exercise program, drink more water, write angry poetry every time you want to smoke, pray every morning for divine assistance, and so forth. And again, the methodology of the seven realms of change is not to "fix" problems, but to invite change and keep the process in motion.

For those who might exclaim that there is too much change in their lives or that they need more stability,[6] try inviting that change by creating more stable or long-term constructs, such as...

<u>Physical</u>: Wear the same item of clothing every day for a month (not your underwear, maybe a bracelet or something), make your bed every morning, get a butterfly tattoo.

<u>Emotional</u>: Massage your feet every night before bed, every time you notice that you're crabby make yourself smile or laugh.

<u>Active</u>: Be on time for work every day, spend your first five morning minutes stretching.

<u>Relational</u>: Make a weekly date with a reliable friend, say hello to a stranger every day.

<u>Expressive</u>: Before every meal say one thing you are thankful for, choose a word to never say again.

<u>Mental</u>: Memorize a poem and repeat it once a day, try to notice negative thoughts and follow them with "Bless you" (or me/her/him/us/it, et cetera).

<u>Spiritual</u>: Meditate on nothingness for five minutes every day. Keep a journal in which you write every night about something that influenced your sense of faith that day.

Again, many of these suggestions could be made for several of the realms of change. Writing in a journal could be considered active, emotional, expressive, mental or spiritual. But I believe this framework to be useful. Its one major drawback is its focus on doing. Sometimes it can be very difficult to summon the energy to do things or make changes, especially when we are tired or depressed. Keep in mind that stopping or giving up something can also be a way to make change, without so much doing.

---

[6] Both common cries of butterfly people

Also, it only takes the tiniest effort to open the heart and invite change. Your reaction to this chapter should be a good indicator for how open and willing you are to change. Are you resistant to some of the suggestions, or to creating your own, or to making any change at all? Good. That can show you exactly where you may need to relax and open to growth and change. I don't advocate doing something that you find abhorrent or morally wrong, just what feels uncomfortable enough to actually be different for you.

> "We delight in the beauty of the butterfly,
> but rarely admit the changes it has gone through
> to achieve that beauty."
> ~Maya Angelou

Some days Death is foul and angry, and it is best to avoid him. He never sleeps. Of course, eventually we must all meet him, but hopefully he will be in a better mood that day.

You can always tell when he is fuming by the strange quiet thickness in the air, and how with every breath in, you feel so very slightly as if you might faint. Death is muttering curses nearby.

Most creatures feel the soft whispers of doom and are able to escape, but it was Butterfly who paid the greatest price for not being attentive. This was back near the beginning, before there was any such thing as a Caterpillar. Creator was so pleased with his gorgeous Butterfly that he granted only Butterfly the gift of eternal life. And since Death was forbidden to practice his beloved and arcane art on only this one creature, the day that Butterfly wandered oblivious into the dark storm of Death's rage was a brutal one indeed.

Death is not hateful. He is not evil. Rather, he is ferocious. He does not fret as we do, wondering the purpose of our confusing lives. Death is fierce and full with his purpose. His bad moods are probably loneliness. His only other eternal compatriots are Time, who is quite frankly boring, and the Fates, who are bossy and self-righteous. Death and Creator occasionally sit and have tea, but they are both very busy.

This particular day, Death was particularly foul. He glided through the forest, leaves falling about him and the forest creatures scattering. He smoked through the fields, the meadow grasses browning and the insects fleeing. Except for Butterfly, who fluttered along, singing a joyful sunshine song and sipping from any flower that caught his dizzied attention. He did not notice the air darken. He did not hear the silence loom. He did not feel any fear until he was snatched from the air by a skeletal hand.

Death did not speak, did not curse, did not howl. Instead he just ripped Butterfly's wings from his body and cast him to the ground. Butterfly shrieked in pain. Even Creator heard him, across the world, and he hopped onto a beam of sunlight to carry him to the scene. But even as fast as light travels, it was not fast enough.

Death still did not speak, but watched Butterfly limp across the ground, weeping. The wings curled up into mist. Death reached out with grisly fingers and plucked him from the ground. He began pulling off Butterfly's legs and squeezing his body. Maybe it was morbid curiosity about this creature he was forbidden to kill. Maybe it was the insanity born from a loneliness we can scarcely comprehend. Whatever caused this horrible event, Creator arrived barely in time to save the tiniest bit of his favorite creation. Death stood there, one lone Butterfly eye pinched between pointy fingertips and held up to the sun as if he was examining a precious ruby. The rest of Butterfly's body had withered away into ash.

"Death," said Creator, "what ever is the matter?"

And Death poured forth oil-black tears. "I. Am So. Tired."

Creator held out his hand, and Death placed the tiny eye in Creator's palm. Creator heaved a deep sigh, and that sigh became a low whistle, a hum of life that he sang into the eye. Creator sang his song of creation, and placed that eye on the nearest leaf.

He could not undo the damage that Death had wrought. But he could use his powers of creation to keep the spirit of Butterfly alive. And so that eye became an egg. And that egg would become a Caterpillar. And then that Caterpillar would become a Butterfly. And that Butterfly would lay an egg. And the cycle would begin all over again.

And that is how Butterfly came to embody both Death and Life.

The Stages of Metamorphosis

Which came first – the butterfly or the egg? In this chapter we will begin with the egg, which is symbolic of the beginning itself, then visit each subsequent stage of its journey, which are larva, pupa, and finally butterfly.

Egg: This is the first stage of the butterfly's journey. An egg is a kind of seed, a vital potential in physical form. It is innocent and aware of nothing but itself, having no concept of the butterfly it will become.

At this stage, you may only have the slightest idea of the change you wish to create, or only the faintest glimmer of a shiver at something shifting inside of you. Allow it to grow, without making demands of it, demands to know what the transformation will look like.

A butterfly will only lay an egg on the specific type of plant on which its offspring can feed. If that plant is unavailable, the butterfly will not lay at all. So be sure to maintain a hospitable environment that is receptive to a tiny agent of change, one that is nourishing and fosters creativity.

Larva/Caterpillar: This second stage is largely devoted to feeding and growing, which includes shedding a skin, or molting, several times. The caterpillar is an eating machine, growing up to 3000 times the weight of its egg. Some species also produce silk to aid in traveling from meal to meal, escaping predators by playing Tarzan, and for some, to eventually spin a cocoon for the next stage.

At this stage, you may begin to feel the approaching change growing inside of you like fire, or around you like an early day of spring. Its outcome may still be a mystery, but its outline may start to become clearer. The caterpillar may not conceive of its eventual butterfly self, but it contains that information, buried inside itself in tiny pockets called histoblasts.

The most important thing you can do during this stage is to feed yourself creatively, and focus on consistently creating change, no matter how superficially, in your life. As the caterpillar feeds voraciously to fuel its change, you may also consume and absorb more than usual. Go to museums and art galleries, shows and concerts, plays and movies. Read new books and magazines and newspapers. Try new restaurants from different cultures. Listen to old records or new radio stations. Watch people in public places.

The caterpillar, as it grows, will also undergo the precursory changes of outgrowing its skin, several times. This is not simply casting off something as trash, however – its body consumes and recycles up to 86% of the old skin before squeezing out of it.

This stage may hold several initial changes before the final metamorphosis, changes in appearance, demeanor or perspective. However, remember that while it is refreshing to cast off old ways, a snake is still a snake, before and after shedding its skin, as is a caterpillar. These are perhaps practice sessions, or warm-ups, leading you to something profound, something unimaginable.

The caterpillar also engages in some natural camouflage and various disguises during this time. At first it may appear to blend in with the foliage, or even be colored to resemble a bird turd. Its later skins may give it the appearance of a snake, brightly colored and faux-dangerous to potential predators. Some caterpillars spit poisonous vomit, foul gas, or even acid.

You may wish to consider keeping your journey to yourself as you progress through these changes. For many, it can be tempting or even natural to share the details of an exciting new adventure, but this may not be the time for advertisement. Sometimes other people can act as social predators, killing off our vulnerable attempts at living a new way, with discouragement or even scorn. Also, perhaps it's just not as fun and rewarding to tell others about your journey as it is to just live it. The simple beauty of art can be destroyed by having to explain it. The caterpillar explains nothing, and is only focused on eating, not getting eaten, and growing towards the next phase of its journey.

Pupa/Chrysalis: After up to five molts, or instars, the caterpillar finally enters the last phase of its life in this body. Some weave this home with their silk, others' skin hardens, and some pupate underground. In every way, the creature that enters this stage will be unrecognizable as the creature which will emerge.

You may find yourself withdrawing during this phase, avoiding social activity or becoming quiet and uncommunicative. In my own life, the chrysalis stage has even looked like a long period of depression, leading to an eventual bursting forth of vibrant rebirth. While I would discourage you from becoming a total recluse,[7] allow yourself to become quiet and still while your attention is drawn inward.

During this extraordinary transformation, the caterpillar liquifies down into a soup, digesting itself from the inside, called hystolysis. It undergoes a kind of death and disintegration unknown in the rest of the living world, yet it is still somehow remarkably alive.

We may never know what it is like for the caterpillar, but our human experience of archetypal dismemberment can be strange and frightening.[8] You may experience the death of parts of yourself which you have never even considered, parts of you so integral that, when crumbling, can disturb your fundamental sense of who you are. Your morals, your method of relating to others, your perception of yourself, or anything about you can potentially fall away at this time. Old or repressed memories may suddenly surface. Whole new parts of you, never before acknowledged, may emerge. You may realize that your whole personality has been a character, a charade you chose early in life, now apparently hollow and exposed.

But don't fear this. All of these potential changes, or whatever you experience during this stage, will show you more truly who you are, and help you to let go of who you are not. Remember that ultimately, when death comes, we have no choice but to surrender. Struggle all you like.

The pupal stage commonly lasts anywhere from two weeks to a year or more, and some pupas will even wait up to seven years for the right conditions. So be patient and non-judgmental with yourself. Our American culture focuses so much on busyness and production and accomplishment that we can lose connection with the importance of stillness and quiet contemplation.

If it gets intense, remember to breathe in and out. Remember the gentle beauty of the butterfly. Don't hesitate to seek mentorship or

---

[7] Unless it aligns and you feel it's necessary. Just don't bring guns and write a manifesto.
[8] There is much more about this subject in the chapter "Death and Rebirth".

counseling if necessary. This pupal stage is metaphorical, and does not mean you should be trapped alone while you undergo a death-like transformation, in order to do it "right." Be good to yourself during this part of your journey.

Butterfly: At last, the butterfly emerges an entirely new creature, having completely remade itself. It pumps fluid from its belly into its wings, which dry in the sun. Its waste products are left behind in the cocoon, except for some which are used in its wing coloration. It flutters off to revel in a new life of flight and flowers.

Congratulations. You will probably feel a great weight fall away as you stretch into your new self and flutter your new wings. This emergence from the cocoon is unmistakable, and should be the cause for great celebration. Any darkness or trauma which arose during your pupal phase can now be left behind you, having been acknowledged and integrated into your new being. May you see life now with new eyes of joy, understanding and appreciation.

It is also time for the butterfly to mate and create a new cycle of offspring. While wild sex can be a great way to celebrate your rebirth, what I encourage you to do is create more change in the world. Proselytization doesn't really seem to work, as people rarely respond positively to being told they should change, so lead by example. Teach a free art class in the park. Get bumper stickers made that say "YOU ARE GOING TO DIE". Get a group of people to dress up as clowns and go to the museum. Volunteer time as a Big Brother or Sister. You can be an agent of change in nearly limitless ways.

"Be the change you wish to see in the world."
~Mahatma Gandhi

Changing the Unknowable

Many of you may already know the change you wish to make in your life. It may be as basic as wanting to quit smoking, or to become more prosperous. For others, it may be more general, such as becoming a better person, or developing oneself as an artist. And for some of you, there may be a desire for change, a yearning for something to be different, but no clear idea what that might be.

Whether or not we know what needs to change, there is a very valuable resource for each one of us:[9] our community.

As humans, we often forget that we live in a communal web of life. Since our shift from small tribal societies to huge industrialized nation states, it has unfortunately become easier and easier to automatically assume that we have to figure out and do everything for ourselves, without support. We forget that other people are not only looking out for us, but also may have greater insight into our own lives than we do at times.

Butterflies live in relationship to a greater community, whether it's a flock of monarchs migrating, or Karner Blue caterpillars and Myrmica ants living together symbiotically in the ant hive. This is a good reminder to us to also rely upon the strength of our friends and family when seeking to make a change in our lives.

There are some simple questions to ask of your community that can be very helpful, if you are able to receive constructive criticism. As imperfect beings, there are some things about ourselves that we are unable to perceive, and we can also have hurt feelings when someone else points them out.

So breathe, relax, open to change, and ask a trusted friend: "How have you seen me obstruct the change in my life that I want to make?" Listen, make sure you understand the response, and go ask another friend. There may be scattered bits of useful advice, and there also may be a common or shared thread in all of the replies.

The second question can be useful for both those who have a

---

[9]Besides this totally awesome book!

change in mind, and those who don't, and it requires even more trust and vulnerability: "Is there something about myself or my life that I should consider changing, to improve both my life and the world?"

These questions are very useful methods for both inviting the seeds of change to be sown in us and humbling ourselves in relationship to something greater than ourselves – our community.

Greater still, for those who have a spiritual faith, is the voice of Spirit, God, or Whoever is greater than ourselves and our community. I encourage those readers who pray or meditate, and those who wish to begin, to ask these questions. For those who acknowledge no higher power, ask the Nothing. You never know, it might have something to say.

> "Be patient towards all that remains unsolved in your heart.
> Try to love the questions themselves, like locked rooms
> and like books written in a foreign language.
> Do not now look for the answers. They cannot now be given to you
> because you could not live them.
> It is a question of experiencing everything.
> At present you need to live the question."
> ~Rainer Maria Rilke

Summer does not fight autumn, nor winter combat spring. The sun does not scream as it drowns in the horizon, nor does the horizon grasp and claw as it rises again. Though winter's night may seem eternal, soon enough comes the dawn of spring.

Deserts were once teeming forests, the ocean floors once mountains. All of this was once nothing, and to nothing it will again return.

We cannot fight change, child, any more than the caterpillar can deny becoming the butterfly. We must all grow, all feel, all die. It may seem an endless swamp inside of the dark cocoon of our lives, but eventually a butterfly will emerge.

Resistance and Stagnation

Resistance is when change is knocking at the door, and you've got your hands over your ears, singing "La dee da dee daaah." Stagnation is like trying to race through a pit of mud – you jumped in to make that change, but now can hardly move while keeping your face above the surface. Both are the greatest challenges to change.

Resistance is useful. It protects vulnerable parts of ourselves, and as a construct, it creates some stability so that change does not overcome us too quickly or radically. Resistance can help to mediate the power of change. It is not the goal of this chapter to shatter any resistance you have to change, but rather to help you look at your resistance, identify its roots and reasons, and achieve a balanced and attentive relationship with change.

Stagnation is frustrating. Whether it's writer's block,[10] a loveless marriage, or a bout with depression, it can be challenging to remember that change is always available, and more challenging to continue struggling towards it. I wish (also selfishly) that this chapter could be a magic spell that instantly wipes away stagnancy. Instead it focuses on how to cope and not lose hope, and acknowledges the subtle rewards of the stagnant period.

Ideally, you are reading these chapters because you seek change. But along the way you may have felt your stomach clench or your heart close in reaction to a suggestion made somewhere herein. Giving attention to your reactions – physically, emotionally, actively and mentally – will help you learn about your own resistance.

Resistance can take many forms, often unconscious ones. Denial is a common one (La dee dah dee daaah). So is rationalization (I won't have to change my attitude if I change my underwear). Our human minds have conjured an impressive array of psychological defense mechanisms.

We can be aware of these thoughts and reactions, or totally

---

[10] And of course this chapter was the most difficult to write. And then when the first draft of the book was done, it took me a year and a half to start working on the second draft. Aargh.

oblivious to them. No matter the form our resistance takes, it is possible to shift it. It shows itself in four of the seven realms – physical, emotional, active, and mental.

Physical and emotional resistance are often intertwined. Imagine for a moment a situation that you would enjoy – winning an award, seducing the perfect lover, meeting your favorite band. Really daydreaming this will create a physical bodily reaction such as relaxation. The resulting waves of feeling through the emotional body should also be easy to notice.

Now try its opposite – imagine being held captive and tortured, humiliated in front of the whole room, or forced to marry someone you don't know or love. Any of these scenarios, or your own, should raise not just emotions, but also a feeling of resistance or defense in your body. They will trigger physical sensations such as a pounding heart, raised pulse, crawling skin, or heaviness.

Becoming aware of your physical and emotional resistance – whether it's when a friend suggests seeing a movie you don't want to see, or an employer asks you to stay late to work on a project you despise – will help your awareness of more subtle resistance that may not be obvious but is still preventing you from making the change you envision.

Resistance in the active realm is a little easier to diagnose: a sudden movement away. Has there been a moment when you snapped this book closed and tossed it? Got up and left a movie theater? Turned and walked away from someone saying something you didn't want to hear? Those situations probably held a physical and emotional resistance as well, but it showed itself most clearly in the active realm.

Discovering resistance in the mental realm requires attention on the constant stream of thoughts babbling through our minds. Usually, it will take the form of a mental argument, often in an imaginary dispute with someone else, all in the theater of the mind. This may seem like an obvious sign of resistance, but it can actually be difficult to diagnose. We can be so accustomed to playing a role in these stressful mental dramas that we rarely step outside of them to fully realize they are happening, and that they are entirely imaginary and created by ourselves.

These four levels of reaction are often interwoven, and giving attention to any one of the four will heighten your awareness to your own resistance.

But what to do when faced with our own very conscious, very rooted resistance to change? The most effective response in alignment with the way of the butterfly is a mini-metamorphosis. Give the resistance your full attention, feed it what it needs to grow, and encourage it to transform.

What is the resistance? First, acknowledge that the part of you resisting change probably has some valid concerns. This is why fighting or trying to destroy resistance is less effective – it is essentially warring with yourself.

Resistance is usually rooted in the emotional and mental realms as a fear, concern, or belief. Useful questions to ask ourselves are:
"What are my concerns about making this change?"
"Which of my beliefs am I resistant to giving up in order to make this change?"
"What am I afraid is going to happen upon making this change?"

Giving attention to the resistance and addressing its fears or concerns is feeding the caterpillar so that it can pupate and transform. Sometimes a trained counselor can be of assistance in examining and releasing resistance. And remember, resistance is useful. It has served us in some crucial way that is only recently inappropriate, like an old tool that must be replaced with a newer one, or an employee who must be let go as the company moves in a new direction. Acknowledge the resistance, appreciate how it has served you, and move on.

As difficult as resistance can be to diagnose and process, stagnation can be more challenging, especially for butterfly people. The most relevant metaphor for stagnation is the cocoon – a still point with no apparent movement, and even a sense of decay. Though it is true that we are co-creators of our own reality, stagnation is more often a symptom of external factors, making it less in our control than the mostly internal influence of resistance.

Whether internal or external, stagnation also requires feeding the caterpillar. As challenging as it can feel, putting energy into creative movement or feeding yourself creatively will at least keep a trickle of dynamic change brightening the dullness of stagnation. As a friend reminded me one day when I was complaining: "Boredom is for boring people." It is important to take as much responsibility as is realistic for the sense of stagnation, and to invest energy in change.

However, there are often aspects not within our control or influence, and we must surrender to the pupal process, and allow it to unfold as it will. A stagnant period can also mean that we have reached the end of one cycle and have not begun the next. Just recently, during a long and frustrating stagnant period in my life, a friend joked that maybe I was pregnant. After eight months, I suddenly started writing two new books, so apparently she was right. Surrendering to the stagnant period does not mean giving up. It means acknowledging what is present, including our own resistance to accepting a period of inevitable stagnation.

Everything changes; it ebbs and flows. Stagnation and resistance will both eventually give way to movement, especially if we are attentive to the process.

> "When a small child, I thought that success spelled happiness.
> I was wrong, happiness is like a butterfly which appears
> and delights us for one brief moment, but soon flits away."
> ~Anna Pavlova

*i weep
because i'm asleep no longer
so much stronger
now that i've awoken
my eyes and heart
broken open
by the slow strike of truth
i can see right into you
and i can feel the light in you*

*i weep
because sleep was so easy
to grieve and believe i was weak and needy
passively grasping at the televised supersize
now i'm gasping and clawing
at this civilized nightmare
prised awake and aware
and daring to believe
the inconceivable*

*i weep
because i can never return to sleep
my innocence burned away forever
my ignorance severed from me
by the holy fury of kali*

*i cry
because as a butterfly
i am destined to die not once
but ten thousand deaths!
there's no rest for me
it's for eternity that i am
cursed to burst forth with boundless love
my heart ripped apart with boundless love
slowly imploding with boundless love*

*and i cry
not because i am weak
not because i am broken
not because i am empty
but because i am full*

*i am overflowing
i am overwhelmed
with this boundless love
and it
hurts
so
much
i cannot give it enough*

Death and Rebirth

Death. Is it the end, or the beginning? No other component of life is more universal than death, as every being will face it.[11] Every culture and every religion has a story about what happens to us after death. Some say nothing at all. Some say a heavenly or hellish afterlife. Some say we are reborn into new bodies, to live again in a new life.

No one can really know for sure, even considering the stories of those who were clinically dead and returned to life. As one critic astutely put it, if they are still living then they technically are not dead and can't tell us what happens after.

It is true that the butterfly does not technically die either but rather decomposes while still alive at a cellular level. It is one of the few creatures[12] known to us that approaches a kind of death so closely, then miraculously rebirths itself in an entirely new body.

We can find this death and rebirth theme in myths[13] worldwide, from Jesus to Osiris to Kwan Yin. What can we learn from this archetypal story of unmaking and recreation?

Death, like change, is inevitable. Rather than fearing and fleeing this fact, we can embrace it. We can integrate it into our daily lives by observing and honoring its presence – the animal or plant that was killed to nourish our bodies as food, pictures of deceased loved ones we cherish, or even the bacteria we kill when cleaning the bathroom. The law of entropy, similar to the law of change, says that everything that has existence (construct) is in a constant state of decay (change), approaching dissolution.

Tibetan Buddhism is primarily concerned with death and dying, preparing for it and meditating on it. Some Tantric devotees will even meditate in corpseyards where bodies are burned or buried. The Tibetan

---

[11] Even vampires and zombies.
[12] Flies also undergo a similar metamorphosis
[13] It was the Christian disciple Paul who was responsible for steering the common understanding of the word "myth" to mean "false". It actually means "story" or "word" and has nothing to do with falsehood.

Buddhists believe there are certain challenges the soul encounters after death, called bardos. These must be met in specific ways in order to escape the wheel of karma and forego reincarnation, moving on to a final death and release into unbeing.

If we can accept the presence of death as a part of life, not only do we live in a more whole and balanced way, but death becomes another friend instead of enemy to be feared. And when death strikes a loved one, the shock and horror may be lessened and more easily accepted.

No matter how far we descend into darkness, pain, and the death of parts of ourselves, rebirth is always possible. Both Kwan Yin and Jesus went to hell, suffered, and then rose to immortality. Osiris was killed (twice!) by his brother Set. The second time, he was chopped up into pieces and strewn in various distant lands before being tracked down and reassembled by Isis[14] and brought back to life. It is debatable how much the dissolving caterpillar suffers in its cocoon, but the parallels to death and rebirth myths are unmistakable.

We can draw inspiration from these stories when facing any emotional or spiritual challenge, and can remember that there will always be a re-emergence from the grief, doubt, or despair. These formidable states can feel interminable, especially if we cling to them, but stories of rebirth can provide a glimmer of hope for some kind of resolution.

Death itself may not be the end. Since none of us can really know what happens beyond the door of death, our beliefs are just that – beliefs. Ideas. Mental apparatus. They are a necessary part of interactive human consciousness, but it is not necessary to hold these beliefs as infallibly true. It's not necessary to take them so seriously that we become fanatics condemning other beliefs, attacking others with different beliefs, or ignoring experiences and information that contradict our beliefs.

Since the sequel to death is unknowable and unprovable, and all we have are various stories, be they religious, cultural, or scientific, then we might as well choose a story that we find inspiring. Believing in a looming hellish afterlife of punishment by vengeful gods seems like an awful way to live. Wouldn't you rather believe you will be reborn a butterfly?[15]

---

[14]Except for his phallus, which she couldn't find. So she made him one from gold.

In my late twenties I realized that, should I live to be an old man, I would much prefer to have lived my life as an optimist, no matter how foolish that seemed. I admitted to myself that I was actually a pessimist and not a cynic, as I'd claimed. And that a fear of hell had not improved my life or behavior, only created unnecessary fear. Over a decade later, I can confidently say that I'm much happier as an optimist, and not any more naïve.

Wouldn't you rather spend your life acknowledging the brightness, the glory and the beauty? If not, a book about butterflies is probably not for you. Perhaps you would enjoy some classic Russian literature.

So rather than fearing death and its unknown realms, I encourage you to believe that behind its door are wonders inconceivable to us, much as the butterfly is inconceivable to the caterpillar.

Surrender doesn't mean being a sissy and giving up. Was Jesus a sissy for being crucified? If he had fought off the soldiers, floated over to the palace and defeated Pilate in a Hebraic martial arts battle, the story would probably not be as inspiring.[16] It is in his surrender to suffering that we find inspiration, in his service to gaining absolution for all living beings. It was the selfless act of a hero, to which we can aspire.

Surrender does not mean giving up and quitting, but giving in and accepting. When we struggle against what is present, or deny a very real possibility, we are closing and limiting ourselves and our potential. When we accept, we humble ourselves and open our hearts and minds to what is greater than our human selves.

Again, this does not mean allowing anything to happen to us, becoming weak puppets for the manipulations and machinations of others. It means choosing to acknowledge every possibility that is present, including the ones we dislike or fear, and if we have no control over the outcome, choosing to peacefully surrender and accept what is. This will be discussed further in the chapter "Non-Attachment".

---

[15] With a golden penis?
[16] But it would have made a smashing American action movie, also opening the way for a sequel: Blood of the Christ 2, the Revenge of Pontius Pilate!

The butterfly's metamorphosis is as inevitable as death. So is the law of change. We may as well open our hearts and minds in acceptance of the infinite possibilities for transformation.

These stories of death and rebirth also hide a secret right in front of us: they are stories. Our perceptions of ourselves, our beliefs about who we are, are largely just that – stories we tell ourselves, influenced by the stories others tell us about ourselves. I am an artist. I only listen to jazz. I hate homeless people. The stories you tell are so funny! You are stupid and annoying. People will hate this and think it sucks.

One of the greatest deaths we can invoke is the death of old stories that only hurt us and others, and rebirth into stories that have qualities which inspire us and the world. Actually, I'm a mediocre artist but I love teaching kids to play with different mediums and inspiring them to create. I love jazz, and am always interested in hearing new genres of music. I'm feeling really awful and self-critical today, but I know it will pass.

This can also call our attention to people in our lives who tell us negative or hurtful stories about who we are. Of course, we should always be open to constructive criticism, but this is radically different from someone who just says mean things. This change in our stories can also inspire a change in our relationships with those who influence our stories about ourselves and the world.

Some Taoists and Buddhists take this a step further and attempt to kill or dissolve the storyteller itself, that part of the mind that creates our personal narrative. It is unnecessary to be constantly telling ourselves or others things like "That is a rock" or "I am hungry" or "What a gloomy day." Instead, we can just be present with what is happening in the moment instead of telling stories about it. This is one of the major focuses of a meditation practice, slowly learning to let thoughts go and find the simple awareness beneath them.

These stories of death and rebirth can bring us into awareness of our own stories and help us identify which ones may need transformation. Part of the butterfly's journey is to embrace death, knowing that it brings many gifts, and that it is one phase of a cycle that will spiral on beyond our comprehension.

"Death is simply a shedding of the physical body like the butterfly shedding its cocoon. It is a transition to a higher state of consciousness where you continue to perceive, to understand, to laugh, and to be able to grow."
~Elisabeth Kubler-Ross

*you don't rage at autumn
do you?
at his predictable foolery?
scorn each dumb ocean wave
that rushes the shore
and smears
diffuse?
do you laugh
derisive
at every decadent sunset?*

*pat the children
on their heads
as they march importantly
to war!*

*let their divine simplicity
amuse you
when they make laws against
what is natural*

*delight in their greed
in their determined monology*

*i pray i can laugh at
the symphony of pain
if they ever
beat me to death*

Non-Attachment

In the butterfly's seemingly sporadic flights here and there, in the general unpredictability of its movement, in its short lifespan, we find the lesson of non-attachment.

Through the slow influx of Eastern religious thought into Western culture, terms like non-attachment or mindfulness are more readily recognized here. Of course, the global spread of ideas has also unfortunately caused their dilution.

The most rudimentary premise of Buddhism is that attachments, which are desired outcomes, create suffering. In order to release oneself from suffering, and from the cycle of reincarnation, one must meditate on releasing desire and control. This is very difficult, considering that most industrialized cultures are focused daily on making things happen and getting things done efficiently.

However, releasing desire and attachments does not mean sitting around doing nothing. It means bringing our attention to the near-constant stream of desires and attempts to control our lives, and then beginning to weed them out. Aha! But what about the desire to be released from suffering – isn't that a desired outcome? According to one teacher I asked, that is the only noble desire. And it is not specifically a desire for freedom, but rather our true self arising to free itself from the mind. Or something mystical like that. I didn't really buy it.

Buddhist philosophy aside, once you bring attention to what you are actually thinking and doing and feeling, I can guarantee you will discover some amount of sheer ridiculousness, which makes it easier to begin finding and releasing attachments.

My mom likes to kid me about the time I had a hysterical meltdown because she'd cut my sandwich into squares and I wanted it in triangles. It's true that I was only a kid, but chances are good you've seen an adult freak out over something just as trivial. And admit it, so have you. Let's be honest here. So have I.

Non-attachment also does not mean having zero expectations. It means working towards acceptance when your expectations are not met. A friend is late to pick you up to go see a movie? Go out for ice cream instead. Non-attachment teaches that the more expectations you have, especially of other people, the more often you will be disappointed. I'm not suggesting you have no expectations at all – only that beginning a practice of non-attachment will reduce aggravation and promote peace and serenity. A butterfly will simply move on to another flower.

This way of being can be a delight to practice, a release from the confinement of largely self-imposed rigidity, control and urgency. But it can be frustrating to those still operating in a culture of expectation and attachment.

True story: Dave, shop foreman of the high school stage crew, goes out to the parking lot, in search of the reggae band that's late for sound-check before the school dance. He sees their van, but it seems empty. He knocks on the back door, which opens. Thick clouds of ganja smoke billow out, cloaking the band sitting there.
Dave: Hey guys. What time are you loading in to sound-check?
Band leader: Eight o'clock, mon.
Dave: Uh, it's eight-thirty already.
Band leader: Nine o'clock, mon.
And they shut the door on a highly amused Dave, who chose to laugh all the way back to the stage rather than getting upset.

So there are some things we cannot control, and some things that would require too much energy expenditure to force control over them. Instead we can change ourselves and our expectations in response to them, and we can relax into the new outcome, not taking any of it personally. Or we can have a big emotional reaction that is ultimately about not getting what we think we want, and which will probably not change the outcome anyway.

Instead of endlessly complaining and cajoling your room-mate, who won't clean the bathroom or the kitchen, you might just accept it and clean it yourself, admitting that life isn't fair. Or you could find a new room-mate.

Again, I am not suggesting that we let others do whatever they want, without holding them accountable, especially government. Accepting whatever your children do, without holding them to any standards of behavior, would be a terrible way to raise them. I am suggesting that, in any situation where you feel yourself suddenly attached to an outcome, you stop and consider what you are attached to and why you are so attached to it. Some of your reasons may be valid. Many are probably not. But it does hurt to let go, and it is not an easy process. Attachments – desires and the need to control – are one of the main causes of personal suffering.

There is another form of attachment that is more subtle, as well as more difficult to discuss. Our American culture does not have a developed language to describe the tangible reality of the emotional realm. There are occasional references to it in love songs and common turns of phrase: there's a hole in me where you used to be, they were attached at the hip, he is really pushy.

Imagine for a moment that each of us has a cocoon around us at all times. Called the aura by new agers or the Wei Qi in Traditional Chinese Medicine, it varies in size, texture, and density from person to person. Here I will continue to call it the cocoon.

A famous actor's cocoon might fill a whole room due to personal magnetism and charisma. An angry aggressive person's cocoon might be hard and invasive, pushing on the surrounding people. Someone who gets sick easily or is anxious and frightened may have a thin and fragile cocoon.

In addition to having our own unique cocoon, we also establish real and tangible connections with others by connecting our cocoons. Again, we have turns of phrase to loosely describe these connections: he's walled off, she took him under her wing, that break-up tore me apart. But these are not mere analogies or poetic descriptions. They are our culture's attempt to describe an actual layer of ourselves that we don't commonly acknowledge.

Years ago, I was deeply in love. I'd never had such powerful feelings of expansion, attraction, and desire. Songs and poetry poured out of me like fire. Though she said she felt the same, the girlfriend was often withdrawn, defensive, and emotional, which I assumed to be her own issues. We spent the entire duration of the relationship in a back-and-forth dance of intimacy and frustration, until she pushed me away one time too many, and I ended the romance. We still attempted to maintain a friendship.

A few months later, we were spending Thanksgiving together with some friends, and were somehow in the dance again, where I was seeking something from her, and she was dark and withdrawn. But this time, I was lucky enough to notice something different about the dance: there was a way I was connected to her that I wasn't connected with my very close friends, whom I'd known for many more years than the ex-girlfriend.

Giving closer attention, I noticed that part of me was constantly engaged in monitoring her emotional state. It felt like I was somehow extending a part of my cocoon onto her, into her, in a way that I didn't with anyone else. I imagine this is how mothers feel connected to their children, which seems far more appropriate than for two adults.

Horrified and ashamed, I realized that her demands for space weren't for physical distance, but for emotional autonomy. I had been projecting into her cocoon the whole time, thinking I was loving her but actually invading her in a way she couldn't express and I couldn't perceive. I asked her to go on a walk with me, and explained what I'd realized, and apologized. She graciously forgave me, and I began a challenging personal quest to change the way I connected with women, which has brought me into more balanced relationships with less attachments.

Sound crazy? I invite you to give some attention to this phenomenon in your own relationships, and see what develops. You may already have in mind an example of these subtler attachments. Often, we feel uncomfortable around someone, but can't explain it. Or we feel magnetically drawn to someone, almost like we know what they are feeling as they are feeling it. See if this chapter can help you figure it out.

Attachments are not always unhealthy, but they should be examined and considered. Very strong connections form between parent and child, but must change as the child matures, for the health and well-being of both parties. Some of my teachers have claimed that we form an attachment with every sexual partner, no matter how fleeting or meaningless the encounter. They have also said that our familial attachments can even prevent the spirit of a deceased loved one from fully transitioning to what lies beyond death.

Cocoon attachments are easily created and harder to sever, and they can wax and wane. As with other kinds of attachment described in this chapter, I suggest a goal of having less of them, while giving attention to the ones we have or make, and discerning what is useful and what is harmful.

Attachments of any kind are a mostly unavoidable aspect of life on the earth plane. However, the way of the butterfly can teach us to let go of many of them and flutter freely as we wish, lest our attachments pin us, a butterfly in name only.

"Love is like a butterfly, it goes where it pleases and it pleases wherever it goes. Love is like a butterfly, hold it too tight, it'll crush. Hold it too loose, it'll fly."
~Author Unknown

Ask a butterfly anything and its wings will answer in riddles and koans. Butterfly, why do you flutter by? Because I am the sound of one hand clapping.

Follow a butterfly and you will become dizzy and perhaps even fall down. Chase it and the butterfly will always circle around you until you realize you are the one being hunted.

Try to understand its path and you will burst out laughing.

Butterflies must wander and they must rest, elegant.

We cannot become butterflies, only plant their favorite flowers and hope that they happen to come and visit, if only for a moment.

Don't ever catch a butterfly and pin it behind glass, for it loses its magic forever and there is one less possibility in the world.

Way of the Wanderer

Usually, I was the one who moved on, traveling to wherever the open road led each time. But that day, my buddy TJ was packing up his car to head out from the house we'd been care-taking, while I roamed its interior, unsettled.

I burst onto the porch, laughing, to yell at him in the street:
"I'm the one who leaves, TJ!"
He deadpanned: "You fear change."
I got louder: "I AM CHANGE!"
Perfectly: "Then you fear yourself."
And he left, and I laughed with delight.

The butterfly can teach us the way of the wanderer. While some species only move from flower to flower, others like the Monarch and the Painted Lady travel huge distances. No butterfly, once it leaves the chrysalis, builds a home or a nest to which it returns. Its home is wherever it happens to wander.

The way of the traveler was revered in many older cultures. The traveler was welcomed into homes, fed, and bedded down. The dynamic energy that he brought with him, tales of foreign lands and cultures, illuminated the often staid and sedentary lives of his hosts. In addition, he often carried gifts, strange tokens to be given to those who received him with open hearts and generosity, sending him on his journey with more gifts to spread.

There are many who still wander in this ancient tradition, whether or not they know if its history. Unfortunately, our American culture only has negative perceptions of these folk: hippies, bums, train kids, or hobos. Though I don't claim that all itinerant people are sacred travelers, I will suggest that many are productive, though unseen, members of society, and that there are many gifts and spiritual lessons to be learned as a wanderer.

In 2003, I graduated from an art school in Chicago, gave away most of my possessions, and hit the road in a van. It wasn't for any particular reason other than that I had started to feel those subtle attachments to Chicago and my community there dissolving. So I went with it. I had no plan, no cell phone, and no laptop computer. My adventures took me across the entire country several times, hitting most of the fifty states[17], in and out of the lives of many good people. In 2006 I sold the van to another traveler, my good friend Travis[18], shed more possessions, and kept traveling with just a backpack. My travels were mostly funded through honest labor and the occasional gift. It's much easier to survive when the only major expenses are food and gas. Though not without its challenges, it was an incredible and enriching journey.

More lessons of non-attachment are found in the way of the wanderer. Foremost among these is the release from plans for the future. Take a moment to imagine that you have no job, investments, or 401K. No upcoming business meetings or deadlines. No plan for career advancement. No plans at all. No vision for the future, other than tomorrow eating some breakfast and maybe going to the park or the art museum.

Sound scary? Or invigorating? Of course, it is challenging to live calmly with no paycheck coming at the end of the week – but this only magnifies a truth hidden in the illusion of everyday life. It has become more apparent in this current climate of economic recession. At any moment we can lose our jobs, our income, our savings, or our home. At any moment our families or our lives can be taken from us.

Rather than framing this as a message of doom, I suggest pondering that, if all these seemingly tangible and reliable attachments can suddenly disappear in a moment, were they that stable in the first place? Family can sometimes be a stable and secure attachment. But jobs and investments? Maybe not so much.

The way of the wanderer removes these attachments, to needing to know, to holding on to the imaginary future. It acknowledges the fear with which we hold on to them, and helps us to let them go, discovering a deeper meaning of faith.

Buddha and the Taoist sage Lao-Tzu weren't the only ones to preach non-attachment. Jesus spoke of it as well:

---

[17]Except for Alaska, a few states in the northeast like Maine and Delaware, and of course Hawai'i – where I lived later while writing the first draft of this book.
[18]Who was SO kind and generous to edit the first draft of this book, and for free. Thanks buddy!

"Then Jesus spoke to his disciples: Therefore I tell you, do not worry about your life, what you will eat; or about your body, what you will wear. Life is more than food, and the body more than clothes. Consider the ravens. They do not sow or reap, they have no storeroom or barn; yet God feeds them. And how much more valuable you are than birds! Who of you by worrying can add a single hour to his life?"[19]

I've had some scares, like when the transmission in my van burned out, or when my wisdom teeth suddenly needed extraction, but I have always been okay – and that's the lesson in faith. It's not that Bad Things won't happen, but that if we trust and live with an open heart, that we'll have, find, or be given the resources to deal with the challenges.

Choosing the way of the wanderer and giving up attachments to planning the future allows the unfolding of the unimaginable. By not focusing on creating the next steps and always looking directly at the goal, a whole world of possibility opens up. Anything might happen. Without a destination, a road trip becomes a flutter from attractive flower to flower, or a random conversation with a stranger brings an unexpected illumination. Opening to possibility will also open one's intuition, which will be discussed in a later chapter.

The wanderer also chooses to give up most worldly possessions and travel only with what is necessary. Giving away most of what I owned was liberating, especially having thrown a party to do it. Seeing treasured items go to friends and sometimes strangers was a lot of fun.[20]

Once we free ourselves from the attachments of possessions, our true and simple needs become clearer: food, water, shelter, clothing, companionship, and maybe a good book or some music. The sheer quantity of possessions our industrialized consumer cultures insist for us in our daily existence is staggering, not to mention how much of it is just thrown away[21] when it breaks or wears down or we tire of it. (At least donate if possible!) Many people have storage units full of stuff they're not even using, and that they may not use for years, if ever.

---

[19] Luke 12:22-25
[20] I do have to admit that at times I really miss my library of books.
[21] And as my friend Mike Joe likes to say: "There is no away." All of that trash goes somewhere.

Imagine for a moment what you might pack into a backpack if you suddenly had to leave your home forever. What is vitally important? What is so special you couldn't ever leave it behind? Would it hurt to leave all the rest of it, or would it be a relief? Imagine that the only waste you produce is mostly food scraps and a little packaging. Imagine knowing exactly where every single item you own is, right next to you, within easy reach. Imagine suddenly and spontaneously choosing to visit Alaska, or Belize, or Thailand, and not having to worry about your stuff or pay rent while you're gone.

If this feels even a little inspiring, I encourage you to at minimum invite change into your life by going through all of your possessions and giving away all the things you really don't need or want that much, to friends or to non-profit organizations, or to strangers. Consider giving away things to which you think you are still attached, to see what that feels like. You can always ask your friend to give it back, or in some instances buy another one.

The way of the traveler can also teach a different relationship with money, which I believe to be at the root of a great cultural fear for many of us. Civilization has replaced our direct relationship of fulfilling our basic needs – such as growing and hunting our own food, making our clothing, and building our homes – with an indirect relationship of money, which represents security and the power to get those needs met. I call it indirect because we can't really eat, wear, or live in money, and if we have no money, we mostly lack the skills to fulfill our own basic needs, aside from stealing.

A steady paycheck may seem reliable, but most of us have probably experienced its sudden disappearance. Money comes and money goes. The traveler knows this, and develops a new relationship with money. The costs of living are far less without a house to maintain. Work becomes more appreciated when it is occasional and the pay more directly covers basic needs. Travelers will often barter and trade, painting a garage to stay in someone's extra bedroom, or gardening to share the food, thus reducing the interaction with money and the fear of of its lack.

Imagine not knowing when you'll make more money and not being afraid. Imagine not worrying about money and how much or little you have. Releasing attachment to money can open the way to more opportunities to earn it and to live without it. The less attachments or constructs that we expend energy to maintain, the more change is possible.

The way of the wanderer, as a lesson of the butterfly, can release us not just from these attachments to money, possessions and plans, but also from cultural programs of fear and shame. Not fearing the lack of money or possessions and living an unusual and unorthodox life can also help us discard fear at what others may think of us and our choices. Most cultures reinforce their social norms through shaming, in forms both obvious and subtle. Our American culture seems particularly focused on personal grooming, reinforcing the perceived need for deodorant, shampoo and conditioner, perfume and cologne, body spray, douches, make-up, hair styling products, lint rollers. Give too many of these up, and one will probably become an object of scorn and avoidance. But travel to other cultures, and their norms are different regarding grooming, as well as many other standards. So the way of the wanderer can provide the opportunity to evaluate cultural norms on the basis of their own merit, rather than automatically following them due to fear of being shamed.

All of the attachments in this chapter – plans, possessions, fear of poverty and of shame – are constructs that can be changed. They have a real existence that weighs upon and constricts us. You may discover that, by embracing the way of the wanderer and this secret teaching of the butterfly, you actually will feel lighter and more free.

This is another opportunity to examine our attachments, choose the ones we wish, and release ourselves from the ones we don't.

> "I only ask to be free. The butterflies are free."
> ~Charles Dickens

No one could figure out how the old blind man knew everything. Villagers came from all around to ask him questions. When will the typhoons come this year? Where did I lose my lucky amulet? Will I have another son?

They always found him in his garden, surrounded by towering plants exploding with colors and frequented by humming bees and fluttering butterflies. He sat in its middle, smiling quietly, almost as if he anticipated their arrivals and their questions.

But each year once autumn came, he no longer sat out in his garden. Those who approached his hut found him tending fire, silent and still. He would not, or could not, answer any more questions. Once spring arrived, however, he could be found out in his luscious garden once again, gently smiling and dispensing wisdom as if it was a thousand tiny breezes wafting through him.

The villagers brought him food, water, clothes, and treats. With his assistance their lives flourished and they were happier. The old blind man never became swollen with pride or bitter with the sometimes difficult truths he had to utter. He was always kind.

One day swarms of butterflies floated into the village, visiting each hut, and the people knew that the old blind man was dead. They could feel it in the flap of wings, in the flutter of the dances. And they knew now how he had received each bit of knowledge - sitting in his garden, cultivating the plants and flowers that brought to him all of the butterflies from the whole land, and every nuance they had gathered from every flight near and far.

When the villagers went to his home they found him sitting in his garden, covered in butterflies, still smiling gently in death as he had in life. Some say that the butterflies picked up his weightless body and carried him to Heaven.

Butterfly Intuition

Each one of us, no matter how stubborn, hardened or jaded we might normally be, is capable of imagining what it might feel like to be a butterfly in flight, drawn from flower to flower. The incredible lightness. The gentle swoops on random gusts of breeze, in circles and curves, zigs and zags. Perching on a vibrant flower in the warm sun. No matter how far back or deeply we have to recall, each of us has the experience of an expansive and exquisite delight in being alive.

That sensual experience is the key to learning the more intuitive lessons that the butterfly has to teach us. The more relaxed and open we can be, the more readily we can perceive the subtler layers of reality.

One of the main components of being human, of being more than just an animal, is our ability to foresee or predict events in the future and to plan for them. While both crows and chimpanzees have been observed making and using tools, they do not have datebooks, college funds, or business plans. They live day to day, accepting what comes, having a lot more free time than us humans. Butterflies are symbolic of living moment to moment. Releasing our compulsion to plan the future not only releases us from the weight of attachments, but also opens us to the currents of unforeseen possibility.

To recognize that our human planning minds are limited and incapable of anticipating every possible future event is to humble ourselves in the face of that infinite possibility. Anything can happen to us, beyond what we can conceive. So being humble in relation to the infinite will allow us to develop our awareness of the subtle currents of possibility. These subtle currents can be followed, and will reward us with gift upon gift of the unexpected.

Hundreds of new age books can instruct you in developing your psychic ability through meditation, visualization, or magic ritual. This book will not do so, because butterfly intuition is not psychic ability or astral projection or angelic channeling. It is living humbly and consciously in the currents and eddies of possibility so as to be drawn to the right place and time for something wonderful to occur.

One day I was on a butterfly wander through a downtown strip of

Hilo, one of the main cities on the Big Island of Hawai'i. I'd already been through the farmers market, but for some reason, I did another circle around it. I noticed this guy sitting and playing with his baby. I was drawn towards him and said, "Hey man, you look so much like my friend David from the Starwood festival." He looked up at me, and I said, "And you're him!" We hugged and laughed for a while. We hadn't seen each other in two and a half years, and I had no idea he and his family had moved to the Big Island.

This story shows several aspects of butterfly intuition at work. The chances of this meeting were miniscule, but a remote possibility bloomed into a joyful reunion. No psychic thought arose to direct me to that corner of the market again, but rather I drifted there randomly and without reason. Joy, feeling without thinking, and going with a nameless flow were all at work here. The butterfly intuition arose from the non-thinking animal self, aware of a current that was invisible to the human planning mind.

The quieter our minds can be, the more we can relax and expand into the bliss of being alive. The humbler our piloting egos, the more aware we can be of the subtle currents guiding us in unexpected directions.

Practice going on a butterfly wander through a marketplace or a forest or some other rich and attractive environment. Go without any expectation of some grand magical event, but rather with as few attachments as possible to any outcome. Allow yourself to be drawn in any direction by your body – not your mind – and proceed without mentally choosing your next direction. Obviously, you probably shouldn't do this in a forest large enough to get lost in or without practical safety measures. If at any point you don't feel like moving in any particular way or direction, then don't move. Wait and enjoy the moment until you feel motion bubbling up through you, rather than a thought of "should move" or the mind telling the body to go. This is a very odd distinction for the civilized mind to grasp, but it is the key element of butterfly intuition.

There is a self within us, distinct from the thinking mind, which can lead us in wholly new ways when given the opportunity. Artists, musicians, and dancers cultivate this self. Poets, wanderers, and street corner performers celebrate this self. It speaks through those who suddenly burst into song on a crowded city street, dance in the middle of a traffic jam, or find themselves laughing in the face of fear.

If it gently arises from within, if it celebrates joy, if it leads to open doors of opportunity, if it calls to evolve and grow, it is the way of the butterfly.

> "We must remain as close to the flowers, the grass,
> and the butterflies as the child is
> who is not yet so much taller than they are.
> We adults, on the other hand, have outgrown them
> and have to lower ourselves to stoop down to them.
> It seems to me that the grass hates us
> when we confess our love for it.
> Whoever would partake of all good things must understand
> how to be small at times."
> ~Friedrich Nietzsche

Children are always warned in stories to watch out for witches, ghosts and other evil creatures, but most of all they should be warned of the Butterfly Man. Anyone can smell a witch coming, and they are so ugly that their black little hearts are obvious. Ghosts are easily fled and can't do any harm anyway, other than maybe making you a little sick.

But the Butterfly Man is more dangerous because he is so beautiful and because he means no harm. Even the fairies in the stories of old were creatures who fed on the fear of the children. The Butterfly Man only wants to share his wonders. And it is for this reason that the children should be warned more fiercely of him than of any other monster.

Butterfly Man is as beautiful as a waterfall in the sun, and when he is near the air tastes of honey. The spaces around him shimmer with every color. Children are drawn to him, for through him the magic of the world comes alive again, as it did when we were very young.

Butterfly Man never speaks, but the world and its beauty speak through him. Every drop of rain becomes a poem, spiderwebs become masterpieces, the sound of wind in the trees a symphony cascading down your spine to your soles. There is no choice but to follow him in his dance through the fields and forests, captivated as the mundane becomes a delight.

Then suddenly he is gone, and you are lost and alone, far from home. Butterfly Man means no harm. He has simply been distracted by some other wondrous thing and forgotten you entirely, just as you have forgotten your family, your friends, and your home.

Until now, when you may never see them again. Was that magnificence worth it?

Butterfly People

Anyone can benefit from opening to change and from each secret teaching of the butterfly. There are some, however, who live their whole lives as butterfly people, just as there are wolf people and owl people, fire and water people, flower and thunder and outer space people.

Meeting and knowing butterfly people has the distinct benefit of not only inviting change into your life, but actual agents of change, whose lives are the way of the butterfly. Just being in relationship with a butterfly person can amplify every teaching in this book, whether or not this person identifies as a butterfly. This chapter will describe the various characteristics of butterfly people, sort of like a field guide. Good luck and have fun identifying them, and should you realize that you are being described, congratulations.

Above all, butterfly people are restless. They don't tend to sit still often, and when they are motionless, there will still be an air of movement around them. If their bodies are not aflutter, their creative minds are. Though this trait can resemble anxiety, it is usually more a matter of enjoying the change inherent in movement. Ironically, they exude a gentle calm when truly at rest. Overall, butterfly people are very creative and mentally active. Whatever they focus their unique energy upon will flourish.

Their ability to effect change is unparalleled. It shifts around them constantly, and they are usually in some state of change themselves, such as wardrobe or career or personal philosophy. Butterfly people have great luck in manifesting exactly what they need at the right time, often in unlikely ways. They also have a wealth of stories about their adventures, filled with strange coincidences and unusual people.

They are usually well-traveled and may have difficulty in settling down in one home for very long. Even when rooted, their eagerness for travel is palpable.

Butterfly people have a strong relationship with wind and with large open spaces. Breeze is a kind of nourishment for them, and being shut up inside with no access to fresh air can make them listless and even ill. This is especially true during long periods of grey skies.

A fundamental joy often radiates from butterfly people, a cheerful optimism that is hard to displace – not that they don't get depressed or angry too, but their natural disposition is a positive one. They also tend to be colorful, whether it is sartorial or tattooed into their skin, or woven into their hair. Even those butterfly people who disguise themselves as moths, owls or leaves will have a defined aesthetic flair to their appearance and demeanor.

Butterfly people are mostly unattached and noncommittal. They are usually generous or even careless with their money and possessions, and either avoid making firm commitments or unabashedly break them. Their concept of time is often subjective.

This brings us to the dark side of the butterfly. Not all butterflies are brightly colored, and not all of their traits are desirable or harmless.

Butterfly people can be notoriously unreliable. While some may have an amusing perspective on time and commitment, others can be totally aggravating. They don't mean any harm, as it's usually a matter of something else attracting their attention. But they may not understand why you are so upset that they are late or that they never showed up.

They may rarely complete anything, fluttering from creative project to creative project, from painting to philosophical conversation to book to cleaning, without actually finishing any of them. They can be selfish, concerned with only their own wants, needs and ideas, to the detriment of others.

The lesson of non-attachment is never more obvious than with a butterfly person, no matter how considerate they are. You will likely become aware of every expectation you have of them, because it will be tested. Essentially, you can only rely on a butterfly to be a butterfly, and you may be better off having no expectations of them in the beginning. You will learn how you may be able to trust them, and what you should not expect of them. This is good relationship advice in general, as you can only trust people to be themselves, but it is particularly relevant to butterfly people.

Don't let this dissuade you from enjoying the brilliant company of butterfly people – everyone has a dark side. They are fun and creative, and they shake up the foundations wherever they are.

> "I dreamed I was a butterfly, flitting around in the sky;
> then I awoke. Now I wonder:
> Am I a man who dreamed of being a butterfly,
> or am I a butterfly dreaming that I am a man?"
> ~Zhuangzi

It's true, it is far easier to focus on order than on chaos. A blank wall is the easiest, or the dark insides of your eyelids. Fire and clouds are more challenging, but still possible. Of course, they are all blank slates that will show you the chaos of your mind.

But how do you focus on chaos? Only in a single point. Change exists in between states, and you must let your mind find it. Return to the spaces in between thoughts. Return to the fluctuations in between forms. Wing batty noop noop, zing zang mum.

We must be change, which is like nothing else. Keep trying something different, but not just another thing. How can we move beyond what we know? As soon as we perceive it, we know it.

Dingle dangle oomkiss.

Are you getting it? If you say yes, then too late it's gone. If you say no, that's closer to the truth. Don't say anything. Let the question pass through you like a flimbiddler. Oop zank. Gwerk.

Creating a Butterfly Shrine

Most religious and spiritual traditions incorporate some form of altar or shrine into their devotional practice. Catholicism, Hinduism, Tibetan Buddhism, Toltec Shamanism, and Voodoo are just a few examples. An altar is a focal point for devotion, prayer or meditation. It may include candles, icons, incense, flowers, and precious personal items. Sometimes they include statues which are offered food or rubbed with scented oils. Just about anything can be on an altar.

You may wish to create a butterfly altar as a way to further focus and amplify your intention to invoke the power of change, or other lessons of the butterfly. Altars and shrines serve functions ranging from the practical to the esoteric or occult. Many people with no religious background or spiritual path will have memorial shrines for deceased loved ones. American teenagers are known to cover their walls with posters in tribute to bands or sports teams. No matter your religious or spiritual affiliations, an altar can assist you in manifesting change in any of the following ways.

Foremost, an altar is a focal point for attention, which is the most powerful tool we have. Just about everything in life requires or needs our attention: our families, our jobs, our friends, our gods, our cars, our gardens, our televisions, and our newspapers. Everyone wants our attention, including our selves, thoughts, emotions, bodies, and appetites. Anything given our attention flourishes; anything denied our attention withers.

If you wish to embark upon the butterfly's journey and invoke the power of change, you must give it your attention. A shrine is a tangible and practical way to do this. Creating a special area in your house or yard that is part of your daily life will, at minimum, remind you of your intention. The more attention you give it, the more it can serve you.

Whether or not you believe in a spiritual reality, contemplating change while sitting at an altar will focus your attention on what you wish to accomplish. From this practical perspective, devotees who light candles or rub oil on a statue are giving attention to their desires or prayers. The more you give your attention to an altar of change, the more you will align your self with your goal.

Do not create an altar unless you are going to devote some time and attention to it. Ignoring your altar will have the same effect as a neglected tool-bench in a workshop gathering dust and junk. It actually forces your attention farther away, as dealing with it becomes less and less appealing.

An altar can also act as a form of sympathetic magic, as discussed in the chapter on the Seven Realms of Change. You don't have to be a shaman to participate in this form of devotion. You only need to believe in a natural law of like attracting like, or that by creating a micro-cosmic world in this altar for change, you are affecting the macro-cosmic world of your life. Your altar alters you.

People practice this form of shrine creation in all kinds of totally normal ways, such as decorating a baby's room to open the way to conceiving a child or by collaging pictures of a desired car.

The third and most esoteric perspective on altars is that they actually create a portal to another dimension, through which one can give and receive energy. For Catholics, the shrine is for directing their prayers to God or the saints, and for receiving blessings. A Santerían altar to the ancestors is a gateway through which the revered dead receive the nourishment of offerings, and dispense wisdom and guidance to their descendants. So, for those whose religious or spiritual practice includes a shrine, this altar to change can be a gateway to call forth that gentle divine spirit of change, the butterfly.

In this chapter, I will make a number of suggestions for the creation of and devotion to your butterfly altar. However, I encourage you to see it as a work of living art, and to develop your own unique vision for it.

Begin with choosing the right place. It might be the corner of a room or a bare coffee-table. It could be an addition to an altar you already have. Basically, it should be in a location you will encounter in your daily life. Most of my teachers have cautioned against any kind of altar in the bedroom. If your practice or ritual work is sloppy in any way, there will be an open portal right there where you sleep, and something inappropriate may come through. For those with a practical altar, who won't be doing any magical ritual to open trans-dimensional gateways, the bedroom is a fine spot.

Once you choose a location and clean it thoroughly, start with a picture of a butterfly. Lots of good ones can be found on the internet or in nature calendars. One might just pop up coincidentally as you set about creating your shrine. While you don't have to spend a lot of money on this project, I do recommend creating the most beautiful aesthetic possible. Is sticking a ripped magazine picture to the wall with masking tape really making something special? Consider framing the picture, and really investing your time and attention in making your shrine a powerful and creative work of art.

Now, with a butterfly picture or statue as a potential centerpiece, think of what else represents transformation to you. You might choose a snake skin, some loose change, or an icon of a spiritual hero who changed the world. Also consider including items which describe the change you wish to make, like a poem or a superhero action figure. Other common altar items include glassed candles[22], beautiful cloths, fresh flowers, incense, and libations.

Whatever your approach, this butterfly altar should be a fun and creative way to direct your energy towards change. Don't just let it sit there once it has been created, though. Even if you are not a daily practitioner, at least shift something on your altar every day. Light some incense, or add some coins to the bowl of change, or whisper your intention to transform while drawing another tiny butterfly on your statement of change. Freshen the flowers' water, rub some oil on your butterfly statue, or spit some rum over the altar. Do something at least once a day – this isn't an altar to stagnancy. The more you give your attention to change, the more it will flourish.

> "May the wings of the butterfly kiss the sun
> and find your shoulder to light on,
> to bring you luck, happiness and riches,
> today, tomorrow and beyond."
> ~Irish blessing

---

[22]Never leave burning candles unattended. It's great to trust that everything will be okay, but you also can trust that your house might burn down.

How I Met the Butterfly

I spent my 20s seeking, but not knowing what I sought. Some therapy throughout adolescence had helped with suicidal depression and raging emotions. Art school, including classes like "Mystical Consciousness" and "Philosophy of Love" introduced a whole world larger than the confined one to which I'd refused to submit. But an underlying despair, rooted in feelings of pointlessness in living American life as I'd witnessed it, remained a slow and crushing weight, inescapable for more than a few days or weeks.

A backpacking tour of western Europe and a subsequent summer road trip across most of America opened within me a sense of freedom and movement, which sloughed off some of that weight, for a time. But it returned again as I grew bored with college, dropped out, and worked as a community organizer in some fierce Chicago neighborhoods. Though this work was an appropriate channel for rage at our complacent society, I burned out as a result of flaring so continuously and spent another summer traveling.

During my adolescence, the therapist had introduced me to a bodyworker, who did a painful style of deep-tissue massage aimed at releasing emotional trauma. Though I didn't find any major catharsis, I did develop a friendship with John, a giant bear of a man and one of few adults who wasn't just another automaton. He had a unique and strong spiritual faith that, through our conversations, helped nourish my growing understanding that life contained deeper mysteries and truths.

John regularly invited me to his forest land, and told me stories of Zeus rituals and magical staffs and numerology, which sounded enough like a cult that I refused each invitation. Though I had left behind a superficial Christian upbringing, I wasn't ready to hang out with a group of witches and warlocks.

But John also told me about a festival he attended every summer where wild people drummed and danced around a huge bonfire every night, and that sounded pretty awesome. I went for the first time, to experience the drumming, workshops, public rituals, and thousands of people calling themselves pagans. On one hand, I felt like an awkward city boy, wandering creedless in jeans among high priestesses in flowing robes, fairies in glitter and wings, feathered and be-skinned warrior shamans, and naked people. But on the other hand, most were friendly, open-minded, and non-proselytes. Many were tattooed, like me, and had interesting stories of spiritual significance for each piece of inked art on their bodies.

I found myself drawn to workshops on Reiki and Shamanism, though I was reluctant to walk around and ask trees and rocks if they were my friends. I also met Crow and Bekki, who were friends of John, and shamanic practitioners and teachers. Despite my skepticism of every experience at the festival, I left exhilarated, and I have been back almost every year since then, as well as attending other similar festivals across the country.

My friendship with John grew, and I began to cautiously attend celebrations out on his land. I met his wife Althea and their friend Jane. All three of them would become my teachers and mentors. Also at the celebrations I met other kids in their 20s who were already adapted to the pagan culture, and who had their own idiosyncratic practices, of Discordianism and fire-spinning. I thought the others standing around in robes, waving their arms in the air and summoning angels in loud voices were foolish and theatrical, and I still do. But I found that a relationship with that land itself – tending to it, camping on it, drumming and singing and dancing around the fire – filled an emptiness in me which I'd always assumed to be a deep and permanent personal flaw. This slowly growing revelation often brought unusual tears.

A few years later, Crow and Bekki came to Chicago and taught a weekend workshop, Introduction to Shamanism. I was there alongside John, Jane, and about thirty others from that community. Though still skeptical, I was also curious to know more about a spiritual practice that was grounded in relationship with the natural world, as ancient as the first humans.

The first morning was spent in lengthy introduction to the history of shamanic practice, and the foundations of grounding, centering and shielding which Crow and Bekki taught were necessary protective and preliminary steps. Then we were to lay or sit comfortably, listen to the simple drum beating, and visualize ourselves moving out of our bodies to a cherished place. We would enter some kind of tunnel there, and descend to a world beneath this one to meet our ally in the spirit world. I was prepared for just about anything, or nothing, to happen.

As the drumming began, my mind moved quickly, and I had to stay intent on slowing down and allowing the creative tapestry to unfold. A grey misty tunnel led downward and into a cave, onto an empty beach. It was near dusk, and up the beach loomed a dark forest of black and twisted trees, foliage softened by the mist. As I approached the forest in spastic stutters of a mind untrained in this kind of focus, a bright orange butterfly flew out from behind a tree and fluttered down a path through the forest. I followed it deeper into the shadows.

Along that path I encountered the occasional animal and forced myself, though it felt silly, to ask as instructed, "Are you my ally?" None of the animals responded. They ignored me. My journey spiraled on through this underworld, over a cliff, into the sea, back into the forest. And still no contact. Frustrated, I considered for a moment that, if I was making it all up, as the skeptic in me maintained, then why couldn't I make contact?

One of the trees suddenly burst forth thousands of of orange beads, pebble-sized, from a widening split up its trunk They spilled in shifting piles, and a throne of stone gravitated forward, flanked by unlit iron torches. I moved to seat myself, but was halted by a sense of unease. A skeleton in a black cloak materialized and began to speak to me. It told me that I was no stranger to this path of shamanism, but that I had made a lot of abusive choices. If I was to walk this path in this life, I had a lot of work to do.

The change in the drumbeat called us back to our bodies, to the room for more sage smoke cleansing. We sat in a large circle, and shared our stories, one by one, of frustration or excitement or confusion. When it was my turn to speak, I was suddenly overcome with a deep sobbing which continued through my story and afterward in the bathroom because I was so embarrassed. During the break for lunch, discussing my experience with Jane, she leaned closer to me and slipped her question in: "Did you ask the butterfly if it was your ally?" I shook my head. "No." A butterfly?

Of course, later that afternoon when I journeyed to that underworld again to ask, the answer was yes. I began to learn the profound and transcendent power of the butterfly, which was its first lesson, that this power lived in such an apparently weak and flitting creature. The second lesson was in the transformation of facing and quitting my alcohol addiction, and just for giggles, I quit smoking tobacco at the same time. It felt like being torn open to a whole new way of painfully exquisite feeling and sensation, and was the first major transformation I had actually chosen for myself, my first death and rebirth. I continued to study with all of the teachers named in this story, as well as others who appeared at the right times. Many more butterfly lessons came. Later I had a large butterfly tattooed across my chest as a way to honor this ally and friend who taught me so much.

I hope you have found useful lessons in these secret teachings of the butterfly. Many times while writing, I've challenged myself with variations on one question: "Who am I to be writing this book?" Not that I question the validity of the lessons I have learned from my experiences and studies of the butterfly, but I do question what it means to be a teacher or an authority. In my years of seeking and learning, I have observed every person presenting him or herself as a teacher fall victim to a number of what I consider to be traps and mistakes.

All that energy of attention and devotion from students and followers can be inspiring, and it can become addictive. I've seen many egos swollen so large it seems to obstruct the ability to hear anything but praise. These teachers become self-righteous and think they know better than anyone else. Some go so far as to take advantage of nubile sexual energy offered by the naïve.

Accepting that energy can also mean that the teacher becomes a projection screen for the delusions and psycho-emotional issues of many of those devotees. Suddenly he or she is mommy or daddy, and held responsible for abandonment issues, tantrums, or any personal wound still unhealed. One of my teachers understood and invited this dynamic, and assisted in healing and maturing many people, including myself, for which I am thankful. But that constant chaos and demand took a severe toll on her health and family, and her community imploded more than once in the short time I was present. It was a traumatic experience for most of the participants.

Many teachers also then become financially dependent on their followers and students, becoming salespeople always on the lookout to sell the next workshop, healing session, or book. Their motives become suspect and their integrity compromised. If we need to "heal" ten people a week to pay our bills, are we truly doing spiritual work?

If all this is included in being a teacher, then count me out. I'm happy to share what I have learned, and advance the cause of transformative growth and healing. I'm not a shaman, a guru, or a spiritual teacher. I belch, fart, pick my nose, and am sometimes an asshole.

I have written this book because it burned through me from within. I am an agent of change, dedicated to the metamorphosis of ourselves, our culture, and our world.

> "Do ye not comprehend that we are worms,
> born to bring forth the angelic butterfly
> that flieth unto judgment without screen?"
> ~Dante Alighieri

Poppy DeBoer currently works at a crisis shelter for runaway and homeless youth, and is pursuing a Master's degree in Clinical Mental Health Counseling. He lives with his wife and daughter in the mountains near Asheville, North Carolina. In his small bits of spare time, he is a photographer, painter, poet, writer, drummer, musician, and friend.

agencyofchange@gmail.com

Made in the USA
Coppell, TX
08 January 2022